IT'S TIME TO EAT APPLE MUFFINS

It's Time to Eat APPLE MUFFINS

Walter the Educator

Silent King Books
A WhichHead Entertainment Imprint

Copyright © 2024 by Walter the Educator

All rights reserved. No part of this book may be reproduced in any manner whatsoever without written per- mission except in the case of brief quotations embodied in critical articles and reviews.

First Printing, 2024

Disclaimer

This book is a literary work; the story is not about specific persons, locations, situations, and/or circumstances unless mentioned in a historical context. Any resemblance to real persons, locations, situations, and/or circumstances is coincidental. This book is for entertainment and informational purposes only. The author and publisher offer this information without warranties expressed or implied. No matter the grounds, neither the author nor the publisher will be accountable for any losses, injuries, or other damages caused by the reader's use of this book. The use of this book acknowledges an understanding and acceptance of this disclaimer.

It's Time to Eat APPLE MUFFINS is a collectible early learning book by Walter the Educator suitable for all ages belonging to Walter the Educator's Time to Eat Book Series. Collect more books at WaltertheEducator.com

USE THE EXTRA SPACE TO TAKE NOTES AND DOCUMENT YOUR MEMORIES

APPLE MUFFINS

It's time to eat, the muffins are here,

It's Time to Eat

Apple Muffins

Warm and cozy, bringing cheer!

Golden tops and apples sweet,

A yummy snack that can't be beat.

The smell of cinnamon fills the air,

Apple muffins everywhere!

Soft and fluffy, fresh from the pan,

Grab one quick, because you can!

Take a bite, oh what a treat,

Tender muffins, apples meet.

Chunks of fruit in every taste,

Not a crumb will go to waste!

Sprinkles of sugar make them shine,

With butter or honey, they're divine.

Morning or evening, any time's great,

Apple muffins on your plate!

It's Time to Eat

Apple Muffins

Perfect for breakfast, snack, or tea,

They're so good for you and me.

Packed with apples, soft and warm,

A muffin hug to keep you calm.

Let's share with friends, one or two,

There's plenty here for all to chew!

Big or small, they'll love each bite,

Apple muffins make things right.

Bake some more when these are gone,

A happy kitchen hums along.

Mix the batter, watch it rise,

Apple muffins bring surprise!

The oven beeps, it's time to see,

A tray of muffins, just for me!

Careful now, they're still so hot,

It's Time to Eat

Apple Muffins

But oh my goodness, they hit the spot!

Every crumb, we savor slow,

Apple muffins steal the show.

Let's clap for apples, sweet and fine,

A treat like this is simply divine!

So when it's time to eat, remember this,

Apple muffins bring pure bliss.

Soft and tasty, hooray, hooray,

It's Time to Eat

Apple Muffins

Apple muffins save the day!

ABOUT THE CREATOR

Walter the Educator is one of the pseudonyms for Walter Anderson. Formally educated in Chemistry, Business, and Education, he is an educator, an author, a diverse entrepreneur, and he is the son of a disabled war veteran. "Walter the Educator" shares his time between educating and creating. He holds interests and owns several creative projects that entertain, enlighten, enhance, and educate, hoping to inspire and motivate you. Follow, find new works, and stay up to date with Walter the Educator™

at WaltertheEducator.com

www.ingramcontent.com/pod-product-compliance
Lightning Source LLC
LaVergne TN
LVHW052010060526
838201LV00059B/3951